THE HOUSE

The House

POEMS BY BINK NOLL

Louisiana State University Press

BATON ROUGE AND LONDON 1984

For Lynne, Christopher, and Sarah George

Copyright © 1984 by Bink Noll
All rights reserved
Manufactured in the United States of America
Designer: Barbara Werden
Typeface: Linotron Gill Sans
Typesetter: G & S Typesetters, Inc.
Printer and Binder: Edwards Brothers, Inc.

Library of Congress Cataloging in Publication Data

Noll, Bink, 1927–
   The house.

   I. Title.
PS3564.04H6 1984   811'.54   84-12590
ISBN 0-8071-1197-X
ISBN 0-8071-1198-8 (pbk.)

I wish to express my gratitude to the trustees and administrators of Beloit College who, by appointing me Poet in Residence, have generously provided time for me to write this book; to the National Endowment for the Arts for its great help; and to my colleague Dennis Moore for his insights.

Grateful acknowledgment is made to the publishers of the following publications, in which some of the poems have previously appeared. PERIODICALS: *American Literary Review, Ascent, Beloit Poetry Journal, Caim, Cedar Rock, Chicago Tribune Sunday Magazine, Equal Time, National Forum, New Republic, New Yorker, Peninsula Review, Poetry, Poetry Review, Southern Poetry Review, Three Rivers Poetry Journal, Virginia Quarterly Review, Wasatch Front, Wisconsin Academy Review, Xavier Review, Yale Review;* ANTHOLOGIES: *A Geography of Poets,* edited by Edward Field; *Messages: A Thematic Anthology of Poetry,* edited by X. J. Kennedy; and *Poetry Out of Wisconsin,* edited by August William Derleth.

"Angel" reprinted by permission; © 1969 The New Yorker Magazine, Inc. "What I Would Save in Case of Fire" reprinted by permission of the Poetry Society of America. Originally published in *The Poetry Review,* Vol. 1, No. 1 (Fall/Spring, 1983); copyright © 1983 by Bink Noll.

Contents

THE HOUSE

Anathema, for the front door

Pass.
   However, let your tongue behave.
In quiet planned for solicitude
we repose beyond questions of blame.
We keep the appearances of love.
We are proud of one another still.

Allow your hour among us to calm
your opinions, your face, your gestures
like the light flowing through linen shades,
the brass smiling at its own brightness.

Be good.
   Else, when you go, may your head
crowd with rebukes. But your mouth be shut
to a stone crack that permits no vent
to your mischief. And your eye find fault
with the good it saw and did not see.

Essences

I

A gentleman near me in the plane
wears a lavender cologne that brings
a child's comfort, holding a big hand,
and my grandfather back to my side.

Ten, twenty years since I thought about
this scent, even in a barber shop,
yet now so accurate it implies
the stale cigar smoke in his wool coat.

II

Steadily our house exhales clear haze
from its elements and honest age.
After she had flown a thousand miles
my grown child stopped, put what she carried

down, stopped inside the front door, shut it,
shut her eyes, leaned there and breathed in like
a small beast remembering it's safe.
She let her breath go: "I know I'm home now."

Emptying the Birthplace

I'm a homemade hero in an amateur
film about an adult moving dreamlike through
the scene of childhood, on the last day of which
I wake before the birds, put on a brand-new
white suit and find myself in the blank attic
making sure it's empty, the closets, the maid's
room, then start my descent through each emptied place
to ascertain that its heart is pulled out.

I sense no weight, no everyday appetite,
not even my new loss—until I arrive
at the cold room off the basement, the last door,
and visit the one fact I forgot: pickles
put up thirty years ago. She was my age then.
Otherwise her house bears no trace of my late
mother, the one who could recollect my birth.
Her only child, I have finished knowing her.

Except for pickles I have not been allowed
to forget anything during ten days spent
checking backs and corners of storage spaces,
soot fine as face powder covering details
she had forgot she put away or ever bought.
What I want is in a moving-van moving
far away westward. What I don't is at the curb
in a mountain of black neoprene bags. Trash.

I close the door behind me. Behind it, air
is closed where parents breathed after me, before.
I double-lock it and in the mailbox drop
the key for an agent who'll sell where I was born.
The peonies lining the walk are sticky
the way they were this time of year, and covered
still with tiny ants. Parents who I'll never
find out more about crowd and darken in my head.

The Inheritor

Twin-framed on the baby grand my dead parents
look into this room from faraway Newport
where, newlyweds, they were photographed in their
navy blues. She was called a yeoman-f.
In 1917 they started married life
lodged in the Russians' summer embassy that
no ambassador stayed to use that bloody year.

Back to normal in South Orange they bought a less
splendid house than that and lived their lives out there,
the house where I grew up. Today they,
who are buried in New Jersey, their souls,
are exiled in Wisconsin. Some household goods
are also here and all their money—hostages to
accidents of my career. They're my best friends.

Of their young likenesses I'm the only child
and aftermath of their concerns. What goes on
in these rooms will never shame them, never hurt
for we have at heart each other's happiness.
After orphaning, veneration is what's best.
Parted from state and oblivion, they came
to be my guardians. They became Shining Ones.

Observe them look from the end of this long room:
accountable, mild, generous, out-of-date.
But theirs is the way things are done in this house.
Reluctant pioneers, they've claimed it. Grateful,
I live under their blessing, sure they'd want to
be no place else except this faraway state.
No matter where I live it would be their place.

Guests

Once they knock and enter wearing
best shoes and the dog has settled down,
we start the second episode in this script
which each has taken part in before,
lines that sound as easy to exchange—
keep up—as acrobatics seem. But
beneath comic ease our iron deportment
provides mealtime with its gilded grace.

When they enter the asylum of
my house and drink my drinks, the dog acts
as if they're just family to flatter
them because he knows they're rarer still:
they're company. Walls and good manners
keep all appetites they left outside out
and show us off in sparkling content that,
like music, lights up the *mise en scène*.

When friends move to table, they're certain
no shortages exist. Such thoughts breed
good manners—as if a trio
is playing behind some potted palms
and the specter of the Swedish cook,
hired when the house was Edwardian
and new, tastes a sauce and smiles. Around
her swinging door drift costly fumes.

When the invited sit down to eat,
what they eat is as inspired and worked out
as the tale painted by Bonnard
hanging above my sideboard, in which
the old man stuck to his boyhood views
about how dining rooms, plenitude
and food should look even while World War II
destroyed the world that lit up his memory.

When these companions unfold napkins
on their laps, the dialog quickens beyond
belief, for we believe—quite against
the vogue to doubt—that grace still abounds.

6   We breathe life into fiction, and grace
       is abounding now. Stomachs fill only
       to quicken wits. We are all safe
       until right after the farewell quips.

Thirty-two Lines to Post Inside the Medicine Chest

Go right ahead. Use my nail file
or comb. Help yourself to mouthwash,
aspirin, bandaids, the antacid,
eyedrops, a splash of my cologne.

Snoop around. The contents of mine
should be like yours—the way women's
handbags are much alike—except
for brand, that cheap freedom of choice,

and for my doctor's synonym
for your doctor's pill, their statements
about the two ways we're both dying
which neither has a choice about.

Pick the pills up. What can you tell?
Otherwise, aren't they familiar,
my shelves, just like your shelves at home?
Here at the core of concealment

you won't come across evidence
of private woe but, quite to the
contrary, of the usual
tyranny of enzymes. Or their

democracy, which guarantees
to every man the right to sob
existential sobs, and sanctions
your bored search among my ruins.

Dear unseen brother, I wish you
two miracles once you're finished:
that you'll close this door and not see
your face at all, the way dogs don't,

who have no immortal longings,
and that you'll enjoy years from now
a small wild casual death like
the squirrel we picked up off the lawn.

Sharing the Wee Hours with Two Classmates
Long After Our Families Have Gone to Bed

I've taken pains to have the backyard
look spellbound—its back turned on the man
in the street, cold shoulder, the way high
bourgeois art by definition turns:
along the street the tight sapling fence
to screen our revels from passersby,
not one of which has passed by since one.
Out there an elm dies its artless death.

Inside the fence—besides my old friends—
ancient hackberry and walnut trees,
black lawn, color drained from flowerbeds
as though they too happen in a dream,
shrubs in mounds, white lanterns, rotting brick,
the bronze Italian fountain *plashing*—
Tennysonian sound. Otherwise,
good gin and transcendental quiet.

The universe helps out: not one bug
since we came out, and the sky at last
floats a big moon out. Hours ago
we stopped arguing about who's wrong
and concentrated on getting drunk.
If they came out and caught us, our kids
would criticize our carefree poise, whom
we've so far spared much to care about.

They can't tell yet what it's like to need
middle-aged flesh to put off its weight.
Who cares what we've talked about? We have
flown consequence so well tonight
we can't even remember of what.
We are our professors' dreams come true,
gentlemen, the flower of our time.
When we pee on the shrubbery we plash.

Our bodies feel luminous as moons—
as the three lighted ricepaper globes
hung at the far end of the terrace.

A zephyr crosses. And chills the hair
on our arms. On the wrought iron chair arms
the first dew has begun to condense.
Dawn waits. The backdoor is miles away
when one of us must go fetch more ice.

Walls

Though pierced for air, light, entrances
they are the way a man withdraws
by simply shutting apertures
and in particular the doors—
pulling the ladder up behind
him, so to speak, and dropping rocks
or pouring hot lead on their heads.
Walls derive from the first wattled
palisade. They stand for primal
solitude where he can't be seized
and are central to growth of law.
Autocracy, ownership, greed
and xenophobia are what
Robinson Crusoe's all about.

Like him, on the worst days you'll pull
that ladder up, shut yourself in
to spite yourself, and come upon
the Self dissolving (which you forgot
it tends to do since the last time
you touched down on despair). The Self—
a convenient way to think but
bodiless, like an atomic part,
which you've been taking for granted,
the Self invisible under
the most powerful microscope
Despair, that shows there's nothing there.
Your face blurs and is everyone's,
like the face of a suicide
insane with loss of certainties.
Everyone else's and, at last,
you feel like no one. You don't cry
or think about being no one
at all but, instead, fall asleep.

Sleep half cures your insanity.
Sleep puts your features back in place.
When you turn the knob and emerge
into the adjacent chamber

where there's someone who looks up, you'll
bless its steadfast walls for knowing
that you're unmistakably you
with Concord walking at your side
and Duty, Property and Work.
Bless walls. They've been right all along.
You step in and begin to talk.
We can't think about choosing walls.
They're the only way we know how
to close our dwelling space off from
the uninterrupted climate,
close families from interlopers.

Outside, inside. Our only way—
common as sight. And our instinct
against trespass? Common as doors,
about which formulas more strict
than mealtime have grown up. Threshold!
The stranger who crosses must knock
and be invited to cross, then
act out the local tribe's gestures
to show he's disarmed and friendly
if not quite yet a friend, and by
doing so he's ceased to be strange.
Nods, smiles, empty hands, what have you.
He is known. He is safe. He wins.
He knows whose floor he's standing on.
Walls change him to a guest and you
in turn to a host who employs
ceremonies and sacred words
to guarantee he's welcome so
long as he doesn't overstay
his leave, the length of which is fixed
by his rank and errand. Also,
he's welcome to all that you own
within that same fixed formula,
which he politely understands
and doesn't need to think about—
second nature, like the absolutes:
the strict no-no's and the taboo
limit ordained for each item,

even ones cheap as ice or sleep.
Otherwise he's won food and drink
and good manners and cleanliness
and shelter and company and comfort and bounty
fitting your ambition or your means, whichever.

Still, at their happiest, your walls
are a family arrangement first—
a house: and inside the house rooms
of course, for each immured monad
to fill with his own occupancy,
one irreducible unit,
the sane you, alive and vivid.

Nightlight

A noise I may have heard but am not sure
I've heard pries me from the bottom of sleep.
I rise against my will, a dark body
levitating and used to night—climbing—
and my eyes, not wishing to, open wide.
They hear the dog breathing outside the door,
focus the way my head lies, on details
in the wallpaper and a round molding.
By the mopboard the nightlight congeals weight
and casts shadows that make me upside down.

That noise—if there was one—does not repeat
but I'm warned now anyhow and need to stalk
and do, and what I feel is nude and brave
to be a hero inventing a house,
a champion prowling down phantom stairs
into a cave where the man-eater stops
gnawing a skull and watches for my scent.
However, streetlight's there ahead of me
and reveals that he's gone leaving no trace.
Dwindled, I wonder at the lack of roar.

What I hear next is the house stretch and turn
after this nightmare it's had about me.
From danger I float back up the stairway
as a man will when bad news doesn't come,
light as pleasure. I lower into bed.
Without sound the house and I draw our knees
to our chests and then, before I know it,
the cardinal in his tree whistles and chugs
"Pretty. Pretty." for the first time today.
The house and dog are waiting to be fed.

The Burglar

Some things gone, insured and obvious. Plus cash.
How could he—coming across the tracks—*not*
have failed to distinguish the truly dear. So,
no harm done. Just the nuisance of straightening up
after the plunder and waiting for the house
to repair its privacy—no great loss, he being
not observant enough to steal away pictures
of the family comfort, with only wit enough
(so to speak) to scratch on windowpanes THIS HOUSE SUCKS.

That's all. I can afford to, so to speak,
reglaze windows. " . . . can afford" and liberals scold
"You have too much." The burglar has made their envy
his very own. How pure—like a hyena's—his
purpose is. He sneaks in to scavenge the dream
he dreams of wealth and eats up trivial parts.
Direct as a child he takes justice into
his own hands. From nursery on, MY/MINE breeds war.
More bound to it than I, my wealth degrades him.

I can afford to pretend to feel sorry
that that's what happens; but if I'd caught him, own-
ership would have clamped my hands on his throat.
As it is, he already savages on
to the next thrills of fright, of not being caught—
exquisitely wary, swift, trained: a success—
while house forgets him. Like me, it can afford
just this much wealth to be redistributed,
a sign of vigor. We eat his manhood up.

The Hive

My storehouse—heap and burrow. I have supplied caves and bins,
my honeycomb. And the compartments beneath window seats.
Cabinets and larders are my swollen cells. The honey of my
hoard, safekeeping, is a castle against worry and creature wants
and wintertimes.

Story above story stack my frozen things, meats, and my shelves, my
toolbox, my shoes on a shoerack, my drawerful of clean
underwear, my linen closet, my closet furnished with garments,
my cold room, my sealed jars, my empty jars, my pantry stocked,
my oil tank, my tankful of hot water, lockers and hampers, the
cloakroom which is under the turn of the first flight of stairs, my
buffet, my cupboards, my storerooms, the open attic, my
strongbox.

And about any of the entities stuffed therein, I only can imagine the
dark it's in, its packing, its whereabouts. Only my mind's eye can
check everything in place. It roams. It makes lists and is assured,
like a stomach being provided for.

Can you find the spare lightbulbs? or a flashlight for emergencies?
the duplicate car keys? the blue vase? the unopened sack of flour?
a clean rag? a paper of needles? my tuxedo?

Which of you knows where the heating pad is? or the Christmas
ornaments are? or where the bathing suits are kept in January? or
which is the sealed box of children's puppets? in which window
seat the toys are still kept?

Where do you lay your hand on a mailing label and twine? a pair of
slippers? mucilage? salt? an extra pillow? the jigsaw puzzles?

Ask me. I am the manager and very busy, an economist and the
proprietor of private property, my estate of concealed items. I
am the majordomo of these sweets waiting for use. Ask me and I
will get it for you. I will provide. I will know.

How It Feels on a Good Saturday Morning

The novel lies on the two pages
where I left it downward yesterday.
Nothing is more important—or less—
than the smell of this room, bed still unmade
where, the moment I step back in,
I come upon myself
in the entire complex of smells.
I lift the shades, turn off the bedside lamp.
Light and the sidewalks are established.
Good. Everything else is finished:
    breakfast, teeth, errands.
Nobody else needs to be phoned.
I lie down, my shoes on the sheets.
That is, I half-lie, my head against
the wooden headboard, the carved bumps of which
are familiar to the back of my head.
Just as this room has all these pieces—
from family, by choice / not much that's new—
my mind is furnished.
    It feels its own comfort.
The wallpaint, the waxed floor,
the white window frames: they may endure
invisible change but without regret.
I pick up the story to read.
Through this morning as if through my lifetime
the genial world pends, without incident
    except a fly
lands on the back of my hand
making a cold disc there.
I have begun to read.

Angel

The dusk we bring the spruce in is like
last year's or the year-before's, many
darkening backward to one obscure
when a man hammered the first stand on
and tilted the tree up this stairwell
so its top showed on the second floor
and secured it like this, with packthread.

While we help holiness show herself,
carols play—albums once more dug out
for this hour, or hour and a half.
The strings of lights first, then on which branch
which ornament hangs best, then tinsel
until the angel, the same creature,
substantiates on time but sings not
nor plays her harp nor preens. The carols sing.

While they sing words we don't even hear,
we repeat "This is the prettiest yet."
Can we recall? Not one innocent
is left whose wish has come true tonight.
We sit in a circle on the floor
as before. Our grown-up faces glow
in the pink redundant radiance

spilling generously from our guest,
whom we've coaxed back because we're afraid
to admit what has happened to what
we once were or at least to say so
or quite let go, though each one's eyes show
that the shelter the house was, when first
we moved, is not what the house is now.

Divorce

After breakfast and you'd left for school
your mother would call "Come look." What she meant
was sunlight across walnut table tops,
on the painted mantel and the dark floor
and the Bukhara's reds—striking its fringe,
lighting pale damask stripes and a pillow
in blueberry, her favorite blue.

She waited there in a robe also touched
by sun (frailest silk, purple to the floor).
"Come look." From the kitchen I'd come to smile
beside her at this shining of the things
she'd chosen to shine and, putting my hand
on her robe, would feel the casual nude jolt
from the place I touched through to. And smelled
the original brightness of her hair.

Enough memories tempt me to imagine
what was bearable was better than it was,
whereas the cure between man and wife can
happen the way a pained mind brings to light
wrong habits to learn what's good for a change
without quite forgiving who did it harm.
So, I've come to believe that blame is smart.

I witness this end of the living room,
her things, on the bright mornings of my life
as if she has died, and am less than half
in love with a marriage that both abused
yet held to in solemn faith till those scenes,
the old-fashioned rending of flesh from flesh.
When she recalls me, I suppose she must
manage to with that reflex of some blame
that the guilty visit on their counterparts.
Healthy, clear-headed, steadfast distant blame.

Still, I wish her the clichés she needed
to come true, come smoothly true at last.
I wish her a prosperous amnesia
clear as early sun to light up the paint
and belongings in her new husband's place.
I wish her complacency: the good luck
of not having had to admit much since then.
And ease from the destroyer that used to
rage inside her wifeliness, that we all felt
but she most close and helplessly while you three
spent your childhoods in this house left almost
as she left it and kept for you. And her.

The New Bed

Ten years ago at bedtime three school-
children sat at the foot of the bed
of the marriage they were born into.
You'd come to tease or wrestle or be
read stories to or just joke around,
and to be touched in that rumpled warmth
where you made room for my feet to go.

In your far rooms fancy me curled up
tonight beside the spouse you've hardly met
and therefore can't care too much about
but who is now the meal-after-meal
day-by-day chance I have left to love
asleep beside me in this new bed
in a room we've altogether changed.

Think of me as a stranger whom you'll
have to decide whether to befriend,
a man changed since he hurried you out
into the damage your lives would do,
a man guilty of abandonment
who's trying to grow a bright new self
that will serve Steadfastness like a nun.

What you think you'd have preferred instead
was for me to maintain the house like
a museum, a dream you'd visit
when you wish. It is no dream but where
the events concerning us took place.
It still is a place, and while it stands
no happy ending will stop its deeds—

or bad ending. There is no plot, but
there's a beginning we shared long past
during which we settled an island
right for our family for a while.
We know how it happened. Not one word
can change, in which observation lies
my idea of Pure Abidingness.

Go away. Don't you see. Where the door was a thorn hedge has
grown up. Magic. You are a prisoner on the outside. Can you
hear me? I'm squeezing a pimple. I'm changing my underwear.
Five minutes and I'll be dressed. Better: I'm asleep. The alarm is
set. Wait downstairs. What I'm really doing is whispering on the
phone, naked. Fainting with love in front of the mirror. Fainting
with vexation before the mirror. Or if it makes you happier, I'm
worrying. I have a child who has to have money that I can't raise.
Is that enough? I speculate on the speckling back of my hand, for
instance. I think how unfair it would be if I have cancer besides.
Now go away.

A second knocking. Look: there's no passage here. The door has just
finished hammering itself in place. And you're right. I am not
alone. My lover is throwing back the covers, bored by this
monologue. My lover is putting a leg across mine and a sturdy
breathtaking leg it is. My lover says that people don't care for
lovers, that we make them feel unlucky. Are you jealous, now that
you're sure?   I would be too.

Listen. In all my life before I've never been so . . . so disarmed. I've
moved to a new village so to speak, not never-never Arcadia but
in America, an everyday place that I am lucky to live in in the
whole world. With regular working parts—newspaper, parks,
merchants who speak English, postmen, lawyers, the hospital,
politics—with the exception of the part about fear. *Without fear*:
the way I always wished it would be. I spend hours at windows
or on the porch just staring at the neighborhood for the sake of
what does not happen or on my bike biking up and down streets
and have yet to find the usual evidence of faction and ill will and
melancholy.

I would not be rude for all the world except to isolate this bed
where two true minds swive each other that look like all other
minds in the world but aren't. *We're* safe. Those loud, common
pornographic verbs like *throb, thrash, pump,* and *come* and *gasp*
glaze over the private and mutual ease of making each other feel
worthwhile all the time. Particularly now: a soundless smile. Who
said *post coitum triste est?* And in a while the nap with both my

hands pressed with esteem on the skin of someone else, with an astonishing confidence.

Still I hear you breathing in the hall. There is the sound of flame. We smell smoke. You are beside yourself. What are you up to in my house anyhow? How did you get in? Oh I know who you are, Discord, you archaic, allegorical, sexless worm and bad, with your hump raised to knock again. Well, this time there is no door at all. Don't you see the wall is a blank wall? You cannot raise in either of us the firedrake your brother called Self-Importance so you can confuse a man against himself. I am unconfused. I don't believe in dragons. You are a blank noise humming in the faithful quiet. Poof. You are an empty threat. You have not disturbed the peace. You have not existed. You have not knocked.

Wedlock

When I wake and stir, he thumps his tail,
rolls over like a puppy and shares
his bright feelings about every day.
We rise and appear like twin planets
in the firmament, Joe and myself,
while the bonds between us equalize
like the huge forces of gravity
that tug our earth through happy daytimes.

The first week he moved in he made me
feel like an ion with a stray charge,
a soul in search of its better half,
which he proved, with good will that will
never have to grow up and brain that
works in unclouded simplicity.
Two adults, we consented and joined
and we stay joined. We are company.

Now after four years he's like a wife
the way he sleeps with one eye open,
reads my mind, learns how not to annoy,
and thinks in the first person plural,
creature of habit all set to please
but also be pleased, who always wears
me down to start out somewhat early
into the excitement of the known.

Our routine is a *pas de deux* named
"Taking the Usual for All It's Worth"
and we might as well live in a hut
for all Joe cares. As soon as we start,
our archaic hearts are lifted up:
hound and his hunter, hunter and hound.
We act as we're bound to, partners that
dance out the words *meat* and *fire* and *house*.

24   We are tried and true. Every waking
      it's the same: in one another's eyes
      we grow big, renew our self-respect,
      an old pair so fixed in their orbit
      year after year that we dream the same dreams.
      After he's dead, my ear will expect
      his sounds, my hand will want the exact
      shape of his head, and my house will cry.

that shapes my body tonight shaped it then. My arms are aware of
their undersides pushing down on the arms of the chair that push
them back up with equal force. I am in a state of equilibrium. No
traffic is within earshot. Nor is a bold-faced worry. The house fits
me like skin. We sigh together. I have put the bookmark in the
smart book that's proving how the patterns of behavior we care
about—from highly visible to everyone into the most inward
movements—how they're not changing fast enough to survive
the troubles we have made. And I've grown tired of its scolding
and panic though, no doubt, it's right. The thermostat tells the
furnace to go on. The furnace murmurs. I don't think I blame
anyone. The refrigerator is murmuring too.

One night my son told me my hair smelled. What had I expected?
Sainthood? But I have no wholehearted badness in me either. In
my bright corner, while no one else on the block is still awake, I
feel the same as I did then. I want to hear the shallow breaths of
sleepers go forth and return. Their doors are on the crack. I
think I hear their bodies restlessly adjust the bedclothes. They
emit muted cries. If you blindfold me and lead me to a bedside, I
can tell by my nose which child sleeps in that bed. Troubles pass
back and forth across their faces. How trying it has been, trying
to grow up.

O shining child! I won't scold, I won't blame.
I won't be angry no matter what.
I won't ask you to explain.
I won't expect you to show gratitude.

I won't expect. I'll let you decide.
I'll let you pick out whatever
you care enough about to pick.
I'll let you help when you want.
I'll let you spend. I'll let you go.

My Pretty Ones, you can go and come.
You can come back. You can stay.
You can refuse. You can change things.
This time you can make rules.

Forgive me. I'll shop and do wash.
I'll prepare. I'll pick up.
Whatever you need me to do, I'll do.
Whenever you need me to, I'll keep out.
I'll be what you want. I'll try.

I'll try to be The Good Father familiar in parables and remarkable, to be envied, who has only one big worry at a time, who is blessed because he can love without doing any harm, a simple man like the tasks he's set, with good weather in his head, dependable as his own promise or the custom of the land.

The house breathes in and out, and where I sit is its rib cage. For a while I am its breath. Beyond my ears, today's conflicts start and take place loudly and vanish, and already reporters are out gathering that news, but the worst news is always the constant underlying mess which we can't understand, no less do anything about and be free from.

What harm will it do, then, if I forgive myself for harm I did not intend? What good does it do my children if my clumsy self is my chief punishment? Whose algebraic idea for tragedy is being worked out, while no gods hear, if I don't apologize for what I am? The children have grown up anyhow. They have sprung like dancers from the insults of childhood, not looking back, and hold healthy good opinions of themselves and survive my eternal mistakes.

So, I forgive myself. I will learn. I will examine this lesson against homesickness and repeat it after this. I will rise from this chair sleepy as a saint whose mind has changed fast enough to survive and be glad that home, past, self, and shame have grown up and may make me smug enough to endure ignorance and, if fact, reach out and touch ignorance, which is my name for the dark places, the mysteries, all things mankind does not know about, and listen to ignorance reveal itself in the night's soundlessness and worship it in the holy vacancies of opinion when the mind rests and holds wordlessness with the same glad gesture that the hand makes when it has tossed a handsome fish back and loses sight of its swimming.

Substance

When my brother left, he left behind
his high-school diary, a book of dimes,
and a belt that went around his waist
but has outlived his size and stays dry
as a seed found in a pyramid.
In the drawer the diary stays filled with
forlorn thoughts that have no thinker left.
Beside them in the same dark the dimes
increase in value, quite on their own.

His small things. They're like my coathangers
and wristwatch and favorite cologne
that can still be used when the last scent
of me has drifted from the closet.
My screwdriver will drive a screw then.
A pin in a crack in the floor is
itself immortally. The family
will sell or throw out what they don't like.
They'll read letters I forget I wrote.

Once the dragon has swallowed me up,
houseplants persevere without my prayers.
A prayer is less than a candle stub.
My wisdom is life insurance to
pay a mortgage off that's been foreclosed.
My hotheaded taste is less than my name
on a cancelled check. My dignity—
thumbless and jawless—is less than my
wallet where I left it the last day.

The Blank Room

Wood, plaster, apertures, glass. A box
on its own bored with its own makings
as angular, bleak, decomposing
as a piece of machinery left outdoors.

Through the panes—soiled and extremely there!
the daylight surprises the mistakes
the workmen made, the architect made.
Alone, the room mourns its character.

More: pocks, stains, smudges, scars. The walls face
one another's faults and few fixtures.
Sockets, the switch obtrude. Obstinate,
the way a crossed eye attracts notice.

Floor has forgotten feet. Corners show
tacks, threads, crumbs, wads of stuff, small parts left
behind, unidentifiable.
Each board longs for cleanliness, for noise.

But cheer. A woman's eye comes asking,
"What can I do for this?" "Much," smiles down
the ceiling. Her mind fills with notions.
The box wakes like a bush, with tight buds.

talk by touch: "We care. We are here,"
                    the way nurses talk
                                right by our sides,
                    smelling like wash.

Tablecloths are numbered among them
                                blankets and quilts.
                    Pillows are cousins.

The ones that touch our bodies everyday
                                are dry and bright
                    and put us at ease,
                    politeness itself.

        Aren't they like the kiss
        when you were small and sick
        that your grandmother gave you
        after she had done changing your bed?

Each laundering linens are born again
                    like plates
                    like us
                                as if we'd never been used.

They are boasts of cleanliness
                    imperishable as
                    housekeeping is.

They are folded away
                    roots in the dark
                    ready to come up
                    in the useful sunshine
                                and open in broad flat footages.

Linens are
                    a steady hand on your wrist
                    benevolent and tranquil.

When the Summer Clothes Are Brought Down

and the faithful woolens hauled up,
once they've had their backyard airing
and are sprayed, then bagged and put away—
that chore occurs at the first mowing of the lawn
when the old people come outdoors
and begin to walk around the block.

Bird feeders are also put away,
the windows cracked open and, at noon,
the front door stands wide open
to let the genial drafts of spring shove the stale out.
Again we glimpse neighbors' cats, we hear
kids in the street, radios, dogs.

This task ends our suffering of cold,
all those wrappings stuffed into storage
and hats, gloves, scarves—the accouterments.
We carry even the boots upstairs. Up and down.
Ethereal cottons hang ready
to use against Midwestern heat.

I feel as if I have lost pounds.
Or lost years and walk in newness.
Our grounds have dropped their winter masks.
Great rains come off the plains to entertain us,
supply the soil, wash window panes.
In the mirror hope is back in my face.

Soon the garden will supply blooms
for the tables, and we will set up
the porches, terrace, croquet court
for fierce contests on the side lawn. We will begin
to eat outside, to make light dishes
as soon as local strawberries are ripe.

The Moveables

don't move. They stay.
When I come back
     they have always stayed

          LIKE the blocks at Stonehenge
          that look as if God had arranged them
               on the third day

    LIKE a dark stage
    all of whose properties and parts
        light up
        & organize
            when I come back.

LIKE cut flowers
that were cut by me
put in the blue bowl
     and the bowl put on the Queen Anne table
        at home in painterly light

          which permits visitors
          to speak in soft voices

WHICH my two selves do:

        the man of substance
    who has being from his bric-a-brac
    each piece true to its price

        the connoisseur
    admiring with his finger
how the finish on every one of his things shows off.

     Hardly knowing where or who they are
          THE POOR
       spend whole lifetimes
       in inexpressive clutter

WHEREAS my moveables speak about my bringing-up
        as precisely as
        the refinements
     of my diet
          or my speech.

These thousands of moving parts stay,
            vansful of them,
          my luggage that can't be lugged,

                      thousands of desires
                      parts of the dream
                      dreamed over and over

          by the taste. They stay
          while my taste
                      deliberates
                      on how to add one more thing
                              to plenitude

    so my life is almost a still life that's been
                      thought about
                      decided on
                      furnished
                      paid for
                      composed.

    When I come home into it
                      I'm glad of who I am.

It is this fifteen minutes, this bringing home—the food-gatherer just back and famine averted—before the food is shelved and doors close on our supply, now, when the counters are heaped with bags, it is this fifteen minutes that the kitchen is rank with fish, baked goods, butchery, bananas, green peppers and wedges of cheese.

In these fifteen aromatic minutes the shopping list has changed into ingredients, this gaudy still life trucked in from the terraces and fields and fertile waters and gardens and tended groves. I know from my nose that this week again we shall not want. The hunter, too, is back from market, tame as a tradesman.

The groaning board does just that. At our end the horn of plenty spills out the two kingdoms, plants that died thrashing and animals likewise dead and pretty as a picture fresh or dried, ground, frozen, canned, bottled in brine, made into links. These many sources of our good are packaged, displayed, purchased; and they perish, perish.

At great expense they have been hurried in from the plantations of the world and are this pile which is the cook's list, the cook's master plan and work, the gist of the cook who makes *nature morte* into meals that fuel and please us, a relief to our preoccupation with running low or out, the alimentary imperative: menu after menu after brute menu.

Outside, the big business perseveres. The workmen bring forth. They make sunlight and soil into feed. They convert their time into cash like me, who's excited by a dozen eggs or one egg, by the sight of raw steak, a respecter of soups, liking the idea of cereals, of a barnyard, an orchard, a civilized man and father and good host laying in provisions, helping put the groceries away while inspired by that next smell of beast baking and of delicate spicery and the warmth of things cooking in butter.

Many Musicians Practice Their Mysteries While I Am Cooking

The geniuses I've put on to play for me want me to feel better, and
for them I do. They saturate the kitchen air and I feel again these
emotions that my people felt once upon a time, and I feel true. I
feel most of all that music is what the house needs, this osmosis
into the high sentiments of one another so I can be any genius I
want, including a composer. One secret of growing up and
staying grown.

My mind becomes Apollo's mind while I cook and agitates when it
hears for the first time details of score and, therefore, of feeling
not clear before genius found and realized them and engineers
uplifted mere performance to this high abstract version of the
actual that gladdens the fumes I make and nourish by. Praised be
the dozens of perfectionists who have rinsed and made absolute
the notes the composer once exhaled for passion's sake.

But when I overhear Sarah in the front room trying her Bach, Mick
in search of the right tenor note, a guest testing his want of skill
on a hymn the whole family can play better but not well, there is
exposed the amateur brown root of music, a commonplace
stubborn as the smell of cabbage cooking, after which occasions I
am always the downright cook tempering his vision of the human
heart while he dresses up dead things it can't live without.

Hunger

coils inside the walls, each man's
lar familiaris, appeased but
lean always and—when not fed—ready
to command the salivary glands.
Then urgent. Eventually insane,
its teeth like a shrew's cleaning the joint
where esophagus turns to stomach.
At last starts to gnaw its starving self
until, afraid his dragon and he
may both die, the man steals forth to steal.
As if I know!

    As if I know how
he hurts, his fright, sickness and defeat
or what his labyrinthine dying
does to make him finally eat dirt.

Even well cared for, Hunger displays
ingratitude, quick to surprise us.
So: buy, prepare, sit, consume, digest.
We spend our days keeping him civil.
At home now, asleep, he's a comfort,
nerves paralyzed, stiff as a sausage,
his tail in his mouth: a sign of health.

Hovel

Emma Lazarus was wrong in that bronze quote
"I lift my lamp beside the golden door" through
which her huddled masses passed, and even she'd
have to grant that all those weary homeless poor
haven't made it safe into the middle class.

Jesus was correct: "You have the poor always
with you"—and might as well have added *hovels*
to his description of the *have's* and *have-not's*,
that bad habit of people to split themselves
in two and hate and then fight. "Always," he said,

since one primeval pauper was turned away
and lay stone on stone or tied dried skins to sticks
or drove stakes and daubed sticks with clay, or dried mud
bricks in the sun, and built his wife a hovel
of penniless stuff but, nevertheless, saw

the fever of beggary shining in her.
Men who live in hovels are not citizens.
They are abandoned to bad food and bad skin,
bad teeth, bad shortages, filth, rags, and roaches,
all the states of rage, failure, and classic shame.

I wouldn't know what to say or where to sit
if I were pushed into a hovel, and one
waited and searched my face I'd feel alien
as if a camel had come up close enough
to bite and I choke on its foul famous breath.

Paying for It

Every thirty days DOOMSDAY,
                              and me—
once heaven's favorite—munching the ash
of ostentation, certain that next
month adds itself to this one without

one lungful of fresh air and a split
second of sun,
                but me—
                          here: my desk
my dungeon—*paying* bills. Panic
like an addict's, murderous for cash.

You'd think this history would have made me
a sage by now, spouting platitudes
against the crime of debt:
                            a glass of
pure complacency sparkling in my hand.

—enough to stop me buying bounty
as a prince might,
                    spoiled blind like me,
in love with a house that's bankrupt,
                saving appearances,
                                    a suicide

and spendthrift
                like me, a silly man
whose goods turn into junk,
                            and his trash
to bills, whose bill collectors—devils—
mourn more than family
                        in the vestibule.

Commonweal

A gentleman of our day is the one who has money enough to do what every fool would do if he could afford it: that is, consuming without producing.— G . B . S h a w

The house floats above, centers itself on, has
grown to be the navel of our settlement.
It lifts itself above the hubbub,
holds itself aloof good-naturedly.
And Nature herself stops at the front stoop
as if we live in a mansion of heaven
and genteel order has a stronghold here.

Outside, the busyness is lovely! Traffic,
small-city varieties of power, pigeons,
wires, morticians, gardeners, getting and spending
so that Nature appears to be almost stemmed
by civic virtues shown and working citywide.
Wilderness is scolded: and untended bush.

Teachers and principals. Engineers. Foremen.
The conductor and his orchestra. All chiefs
and authorities. Police, judge, lawyers too.
Order flourishes in local history.
That's how my house perfects the city,
a summary of customs that all aspire to
where, floating above work, you are at liberty.

In turn the commonweal makes sure my house lasts,
brings into being the nice laws of the house
where the vigorous tasks happen out of sight
and workaday troubles are not allowed.
Friends and family do exactly what they please.
The house is a way for the city to flower.
Neither life can do without the other.

Out there, decisions are made by the thousands.
In the street a victim is tidied away.
Factory   Bank   Office   Store   Agency   Yard
Salesroom   Station   Studio   Shop   Restaurant

Newspaper Lab Market Library Foundry Desk.
Their workplace. Cursed with work, persons are as good
as you can expect, foiled in their dream of rest.

Busses make their vaporous rounds. The mailman
delivers. The garbageman taketh away.
The house adds airs and graces. Its door closes.
Inside its accounts are balanced and persons
can rest in peace, have what they need. Order here
magnifies. No bad feeling annoys or is
thinkable. Time has been made absolutely free.

The Walkways

if filmed the way they do a flower
while it unfolds—from above, one frame
every few minutes during a day—
and then projected at normal speed
so that we'd be looking down on them,
the walkways would open and look brisk
like paths around anthills. And the dog
on the soundtrack would bark without stop
and each door repeat its own hinge sound
in an endless squeal as they open

for cylinders of the salt that makes
water soft, for milk and packages
and laundryman and upholsterer
who's brought the sofa back, men at dawn
who carry out our trash, people who
sell door to door and the paper boy.
And the boy who shoveled walks and stands
at the blue front door and hefts the brass
knocker the shape and size of a hand
to collect his pay. And for Leroy
the postman who rarely knocks the way
he does today and stops to collect
2¢ postage due. And once a month
the meter reader lets himself in.

Like the ground crew that surround a jet,
each crewman doing everyday jobs,
they make safe and ready the giant queen.
They hurry up like Keystone Cops
and the dog goes crazy and you watch,
from an upstairs window. The walkways
you know are there emerge from new snow.

The walkways are racing with workmen
like members of a surgical team
in a film about repairing ills
speeded up to make us smile at ills
and at hale and comic repairmen
and quickness with the hardware of repair:

a ladder with a window washer
or an eaves cleaner with a bucket
high up on it, and up on the roof
with his brushes the quaint chimney sweep,
the operator who knows how to
steam-clean rugs behind his fierce machine,
and like chthonic gods the furnace man
going down with his salvation kit
and Frank the plumber who arrives with
instruments that give old pipes new life.
Wrenches, trowels, the electrician's
box that he rattles around in, nails,
wire, wallpaper, poisons for vermin,
saw and sawhorse, a door being planed,
new oven being eased into place,
fabric on the decorator's knee.

They show up. They're like the entourage
of a pretty face whose name has been
a household word more than forty years
and who they ease into place and who
pays her only friends left, the old gang
of them—her designer, her dresser,
her make-up man, her writer, her coach,
director, arranger, manager,
the guys on lights, cameras and fanfare—
an army of friends that make her work.
How she does in the blare and the blaze!
She takes your breath away when she starts
and you ask, "How does she manage it?"
and this is the secret way she does,
no expense spared in the time-lapse months.
And the house—still in her prime—invents
for the first time the routines you saw
and words to the tunes she sang way back
while you were growing up, and you thrill
for a long while that she is just how
you always remember her tonight.

Having Lawn

From my front porch I notice the Palmers, man
and wife, clipping and edging, extirpating,
kneeling, spreading poisons, setting sprinklers out.
After two lifetimes they mistake trouble for

crabgrass and what home is for a six-year-old's
crayon of a box set on a waxy lot.
They've never bitten off more than they could chew,
those two. Each spring I watch them approximate

this selfsame Perfect, driven on by standards
of refinement set by ladies' magazines.
They have shrunk into being their own hired help.
Whereas I think having lawn is easy as

keeping windowpanes clean enough so you can
readily discern a boy fixing his bike
or me in the backyard brushing out the dog
or neighbors keeping up their yards well enough,

not those wedlocked greenskeepers who think heaven
is paved with overfed turf like a golf course
and who spend spring twilights frenzied by fancies
of some universal mess coming to life.

My serfs tend our carefree lawn in a good style
that won't call anyone's attention to lawn
but house, the splendid face of the house, the way
a necklace will set off the face of a wife.

The house by this time has lived through major truths
and verified even very savage ones.
She looks back at you. She knows how to live right.
That's why, the time the grass behind us grew knee high,

I complained just like Ruth Palmer would, and asked
the town to mow down at the owner's expense
(we have an ordinance) this rudeness ruining
our block, and had concord forcibly restored.

The Cleaning Woman

In a perfume of waxes the house waits
like a lady for the florist to bring what she ordered
and for the photographer—eager to sit down
and pose, arranging the folds of her dress,
patting her hair, each petal perfect.
Just this second, Vergie has shut the door.

Things are put where they belong before she leaves.
Early Thursdays she arrives with work
on her tidy mind, and works up an inspired uproar.
She vacuums and rubs, she shines, she shoves
and shoves back, picks up and puts back, and dusts
and knocks and plumps up and changes rags.

Before she's halfway home blights begin,
films adhere, insects lay their eggs, stains set.
Busy with other days the cleaning woman forgets
how her vision wilts and fades, and that the house
fears it will begin again to perish
from one week more of being lived in.

The house stares straight ahead and feels
the purposes of chaos being served, a nightmare
of more than dust and clutter, actual horror
at tick and tock, its secondhand things
gnawed away, a sign SOLD, scrub growth,
sinking, a cellar hole, speechlessness.

Then its windows wake, and the house resumes
its hovering betwixt use and beauty
like a mother who's thought a long while
about how poised she wants her grown-up son
to bear in mind she was—on Thursdays—
when he picks up this picture of her at this age.

Sanitary Engineering

Every house in town
          this dreadful proximity
                    of fresh and filth:
          the glassful of water
          that turns to urine
                    and is flushed away.

Of the life-giving spigots on each floor
          and tubs and sinks they splash in,
                    of drains and vents
          and veins in my walls, my pipes—
                    the plumber is master.

                    A secret force of experts
          are the gauge masters,
                    masters of huge valves
                    and town waterworks
          and wide-bore pipes
that bring the potable,
                    and sewers
to carry off the foul.

                    One century ago
          politicians thought hard
about wholesomeness
                    and the properties of water
          in vast new metropolitan supplies,
so had invented all there was needed to invent:
                    hydraulics and traps,
                    reservoirs and ways,
                              tanks,
                              conduits,
                              systems,
          the siphon water closet,
          the all-important vent,
                    and toxic agents.
They outshone the Romans, those builders,
and left us safer than men had been before.

Like gods
we leave our domiciles—
                    our mouths germfree,
                    skin and hair shining,
        the bureaus behind us
                stuffed
                with fresh laundry,
        every surface scrubbed,
        every cranny fit,
                    the kitchen's virginity restored.

The prospect from the front porch
        is a dream of public health
                        come true:
                the air taintless
                not a rat
                or midden pile in view
                not one dungheap
                not one refuse hole
        not a colony of maggots.

Our noses take it for granted
        that no neighborhood jakes
                occupies
                the stand of shrubs
                        across the street
        or that no epidemic
                waits
                        at the curb.

The Dressing Room

is the smallest room
the most private in the house,
takes me from the naked
to the presentation self
thought-out and dear
—is a function of
my dazzled vanity.

I suck in my gut,
then turn sideways
to the full-length mirror
so the boy in me can look
at what he loved and loves still
without reserve.
I think of myself as a still
sexy man, yet the boy
chooses not to look long
at what, ten years ago,
set infatuation on foot.
Except for my truelove, who
that I want to give it to
wants my sex? At such a moment
of keen discovery
life strikes me as much too long.

My most successful fantasy is *dignity*.
To exit from this little room
I dress up my stubborn nudity
in magisterial disguises:
stuffs from remote mills,
tailoring by serene old houses,
shoes that cost a week's pay,
neckties that exert authority.

—dress up my immortal part, the *id*,
in that mild ostentation
of the upper class. After all,
who else has dressing rooms?
I'll walk out Correct. Privileged.
Ordained. On occasion Sumptuous.

But that little he, the *id*:
not for one whole day has he felt
satisfied, ever—rampaging beneath
the costume of my education.

Now, once I exit, for hours
I play all the harmonies
of my good breeding, that cheer,
that careless charm, that need
to be attractive and unfaithful,
amorous innuendo toward everyone,
hitting the high C's of urbanity.

At the end there is no deserving,
no silly falling in love,
just the power of garments,
just flattering good manners
to make me feel good—
and proper, too—despite
the deadend of my errant lust.
Even my little *he* has tried
to behave as good as
a Victorian boy
although he gave me away
in the urgent roving
of our mutual eye.

Back home I hang clothes up,
toss deposits in the dirty wash.
The littlest room has turned
into the undressing room.
Within two minutes I am smiling
at this brute having to be bathed,
requiring love that does not blink.
And I count myself a lucky man,
for in the next room such truelove waits,
that other *id* lurking and focused.
I smell myself and, like everyone else,
like the smell I am. Yes. I like
this being back to undressedness.
I am relieved as well
that now the vain boy
is to be slaked at last.

The Leak

is evidence

               that evil has struck
               unnatural as a bear
               or a typhoon in a house

       Freshets rise and spread
       by an evil design
               like acts of God

sill   ceiling   wallpaper   cushion   rug   books

       are wet
       things that are never wet!

       things that rot
               the bottoms of the draperies
               legs of tables
       stand in a puddle

the puddle seeps into remote footings
               and weakens remote footings

       but I say water should be contained in a
tub   or   jar   or   bowl   or   sink   or   standpipe

a gland swollen   hard as stone
               has ruptured

                     and I experience panic

      It's like a cave-in in a termite hill
           I mobilize intelligence
               call a crew

Mostly, however, I experience weariness
and the low-grade fever of worry
               caused by the wearing out
                 of all my things

       I am sick and tired.

       What I thought of
       as solid as a cave
       for the years of my age

has mortal holes in it
hypocritical weaknesses
stresses and secrets

a restless shell of a thing that leaves me
blind and
unsafe.

The Outcast

What would it be like this afternoon to
stand across the street and watch another
man in my place shut the curtains? And suppose
it's two years to the day since moving
men condensed my household goods to half a
vanload, leaving me surprised at how I'd
managed such refinement from so little,
leaving me bare radiators which I
sat on, wrong at heart, by no means ready,
able or disposed to be supplanted.
What would it be like to come back on the
anniversary of that mistake, and
watch a hypothetical usurper
shutting curtains earlier than I would?
I would hate him, that barbarian whose
tasteless ownership has sent away to
die my Free Will, Right Reason, and right to
choose and dominate and bring to flowering
at long last my residential vision.

At this fancied minute routine longings
force themselves on me again like fresh life.
Standing opposite the house, I want to
go on, make the thousandth choice concerning
placement, upkeep, bold particulars and
shape and price that should be mine to have my
own way with, the way I made each other
choice till then and laid a living mantle
of intelligence on every surface.
Those years sweet Civility invaded
room upon room so resentment would be
over quickly like the rains of April.
Afterward our happiness would break through.
Like Isaiah's Saving Remnant we would
feel again the force of high consciousness
summed up in us. Never was there malice.
Never one of us oppressed the other
by his or her mean desire to damage.
Or at least I like to think we didn't.

Anyway, the cells of Civility's
living mantle dried away two years since.
Since then, air has scattered its little dust.

Not that I could buy it back, no more than
I could be a schoolboy walking up the
front walk of the house that I grew up in.
This house lives in a visionary world
that stays before, in spite of, after, during
and above its blinding or frequent faults.
So, my house—or that which was mine—rises
out of griefs, the same now down to the last nail
but a grange in romance, always moonlit.
I, who am its ghost, in daylight see it
whole for the first full time and forever.

I would be erased. Those *arrivistes* won't
think of us, sequestered in their vulgar
roomfuls of new furnishings and manners.
They'll never know that this is not their place.
But after I sold, I'd be that ghost, me
idle and translated into some thin
element, breathing ether as the saints do,
not a care in the world but no world either,
no work to do, no specifications,
no attachment to essential matter.
What would it be like this afternoon to
stand across the street and not lay my hand on
one choice I could still care about making?

What I Would Save in Case of Fire

First the finches. Pictures of my tutelary parents next. Then
whatever I could gather up—the screen of *lapis lazuli*, the
sterling punch bowl, my jewelry box. Who knows what frantic
else? One thing looks as precious and forlorn as any other.
Something crazy: maybe I'd have time to carry out the pair of
Sheraton side chairs.

On the lawn I'd sit in one of them and watch the house cremate the
privacy we cherished. The house might look stricken, as if she'd
just been told she has terminal cancer. Before my eyes the
architect's idea of how she should look, pretty as a yacht, is
disappearing into whatever photographs of the house survive. I
feel as helpless as when my dog died.

The firemen order me off my land, which they think is theirs now.
They are far too late but smash glass anyhow and pour Niagaras
in to double ruination. The house also has become theirs, and
they make the most of it, shouting heroically, acting brave. It is
their theater. The bright paint blackens dramatically.

I move way back and begin to know what will never be replaced. I
will miss the Lalique and Baccarat, the busted Rosenthal and
Spode, collection of nudes, my thirty-year-old Harris Tweed,
wine cellar, the Scalamandre chintz ablaze, the children's books
(in a side attic eight bags full) and the silk quilt Grandma Noll
made, and her sisters, a hundred years ago.

It looks like greed, caught up in the luxury of ownership. But it isn't.
It's homesickness that is taking the form of a catalog for a way of
life achieved and ending, each thing thought out so that property
incarnated heart's desire. All my belongings go and become
spirits.

So I feel rotten that the bed I was born in has gone up in flames, or
that my other grandmother's blue and white mixing bowls are in
smithereens in the space which was the kitchen where we ate
breakfast all those years. Not in my lifetime will I submit again by
chance to this uncommon pain.

The Window

This day as usual the corner of Church
and Emerson is in place, my *patria*
and source of my everyday intelligence—
to which place no matter how far I travel
I return through the last memorized turnings.

Looking out gives me lots to think about—all
the nuances of change we have no names for
weather   seasons   neighborhood   and passersby
the daily satisfactions the globe affords,
happiness observed and happily pursued.

The corner keeps me knowing who I am.

Maybe tomorrow it will be blown away
by one of the bombs our planners planned would come:
light   surprise   firestorm   (whatever we are told).
Sitting where the window was I shall vanish
into a countywide universe of death. . . .

Or may sit here out of earshot in a house
no longer connected to the wires and pipes
of civil life or warehouse, no messages,
schools empty, hospitals unsupplied, last crimes
accomplished under a twilight of ashes.

Mankind starves. Our roads lead to the edges where
life is going on not at all as usual.
For life, on terms we will never imagine,
will poke itself into the ruins of our
brief history.

Air will still move. Sun blaze. Streams run.

The rudiments. The ruins pass from knowledge
while forces of air and dust provide slowly.

Shutting the Curtains

The same sequence as the night before,
window by window the same two sounds:
the cords pulleying inside the rods,
the clicking of knobs against plaster
till the black glass glare is out of sight.
Now the first floor takes its nighttime shape
quiet in proportion and tidy
as if what could happen today has
and we are here, together at last,
the selves stretched as we wish and faces
involved in visible harmony.
If someone passing could imagine
our hidden needs, the lamplight at rest
on surfaces, their finish, their age
he would grow homesick with jealousy.
This our waking is not finished but floats
on into supreme intimacies
of our household closed upon itself.

The Lock

remembers the first door, on which
it was the first bolt shot forward
and declares "You are somewhat bad,
Mankind." And I say "These are mine."

She calls down "Have you locked the door?"
Habit, same as owning a moat:
"Have you filled the moat?"

                  Two or three
bad men pollute the neighborhood—
pillage, arson, mutilation, rape—
and around us the stagnant moat.

And the stranger locked out who could
help himself to fruit and a drink,
nap on the couch, walk off with a spoon.
Of course I've locked the door.

                    But think:
those raised floors—pavilions sideless
and grass-roofed—where villages sleep
without knowing they own so much
that Want prowls forward through the murk.
O Happy Savages!
                But we
northern men for ten thousand years
have bred attack into the dogs
that sleep by our fires, leap and SNAP!
like the more recent, more certain lock.

O Efficacious Lock!   your wedge,
your spring, your admirable wards,
your keyhole and my key and this,
the inside bolt, and all is safe.
Stranger Want does not hear your snap
but expects you, your counterforce,
my door stubborn as a policeman
with prudence on its side, and law.

Now the family is circumscribed
and sleeps, selfish as the spender
multiplying his cherished things.
Through invisible terror we sleep
while Privacy guards beside the lock
ready to shoot Curiosity
in the white of its nasty eye.
O Nervous Privacy! My women,
their modesty is also kept.
The perils of Generosity!
which begins at home. "These are mine."

The first one down twists back the knob.
One more night of chance charity
avoided. The lock falls asleep.
The lock has not made me feel good,
only intact—like my purchases.
I have not honored the unknown
nor allowed the curious to know.